[redacted]

P9-DBS-843

DEC 1998

DISCARD

ORLAND PARK PUBLIC LIBRARY
AILEEN S. ANDREW MEMORIAL
14760 PARK LANE
ORLAND PARK, ILLINOIS 60462
349-8138

DEMCO

Seven Stars More!

Kathy Mallat

Walker and Company New York

Abby isn't tired . . .

so she counts the sheep nearby.

"1, 2, 3, 4,

5, 6, 7, more."

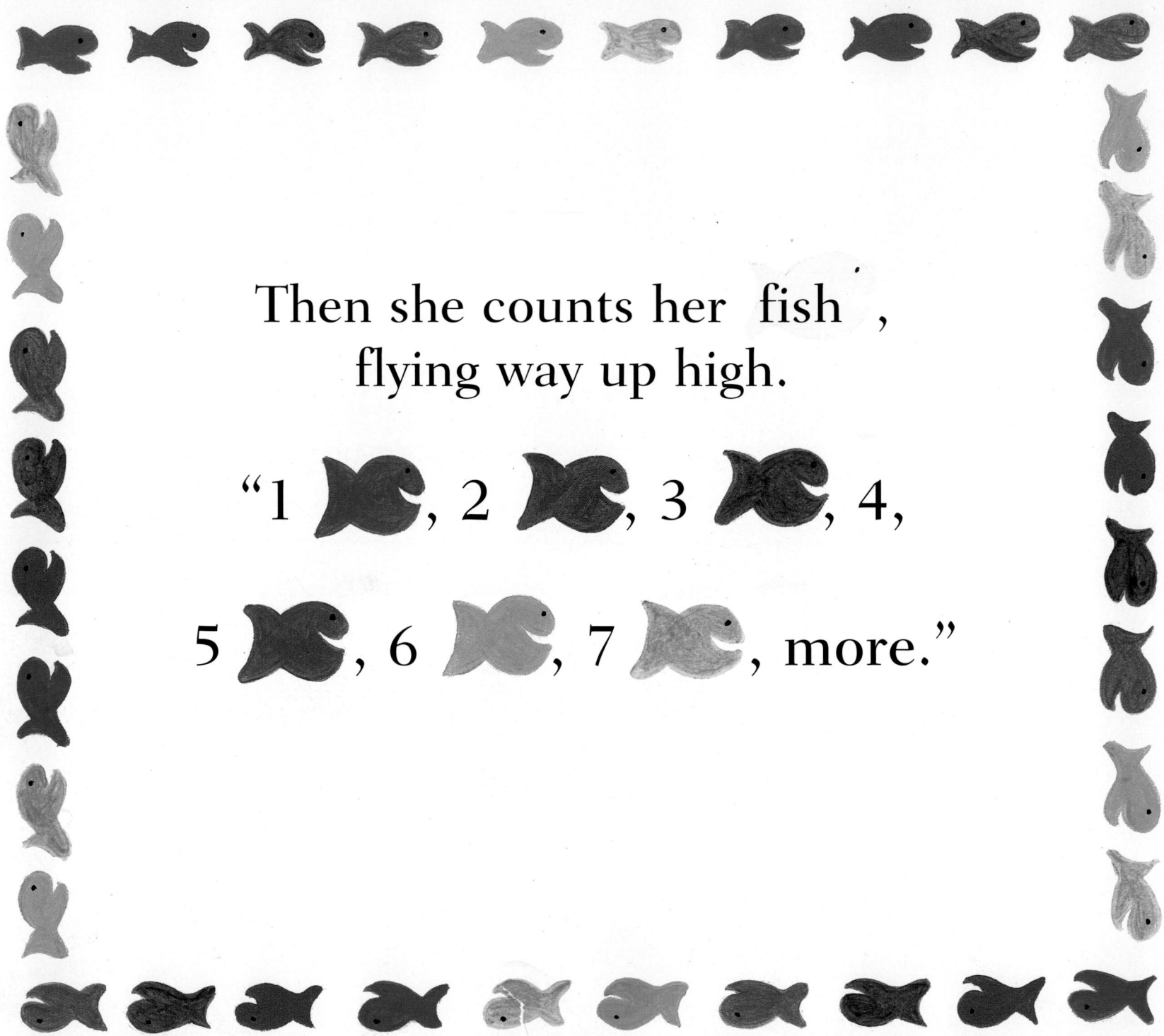

Then she counts her fish,
flying way up high.

"1, 2, 3, 4,

5, 6, 7, more."

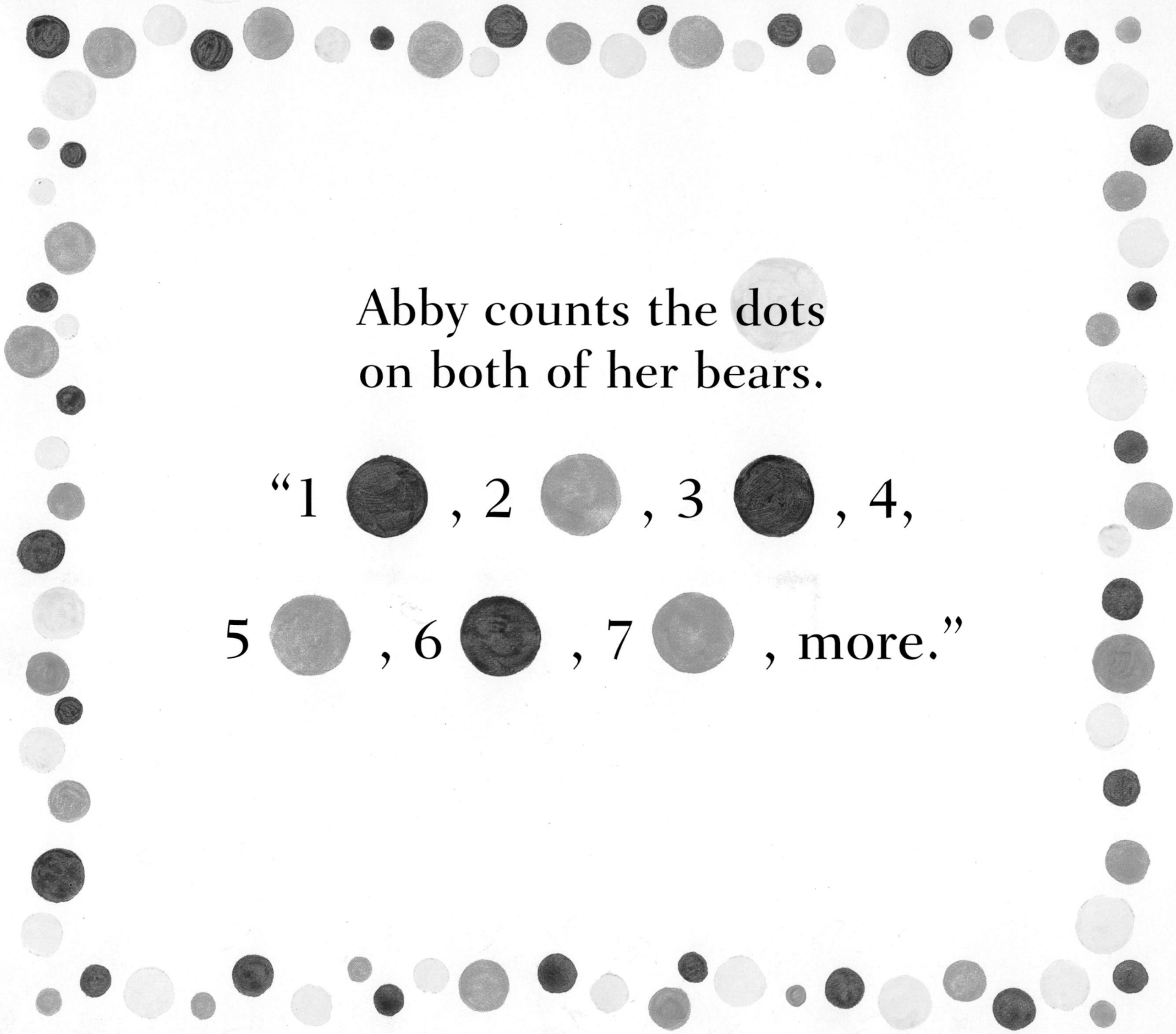

Abby counts the dots
on both of her bears.

"1 , 2 , 3 , 4,

5 , 6 , 7 , more."

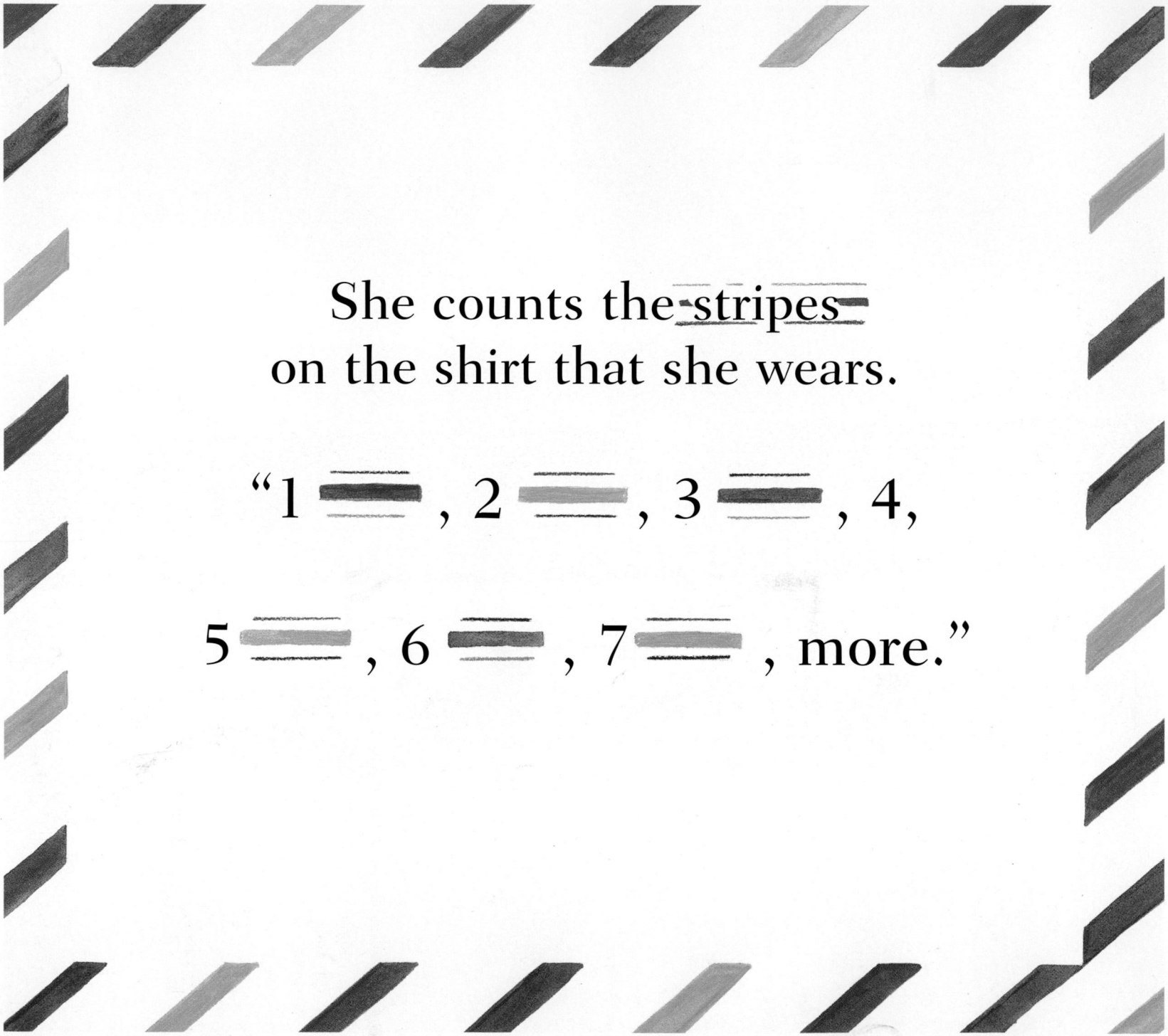

She counts the stripes
on the shirt that she wears.

"1, 2, 3, 4,

5, 6, 7, more."

Abby counts the books
that she has just read.

"1, 2, 3, 4,

5, 6, 7, more."

ORLAND PARK PUBLIC LIBRARY

2765449

ORLAND PARK PUBLIC LIBRARY

She counts her leaves
scattered next to the bed.

"1, 2, 3, 4,

5, 6, 7, more."

She counts her puppets
as they dance and spin.

"1, 2, 3, 4,
5, 6, 7, more."

Then Abby counts her toes,
and tucks them in.

"1, 2, 3, 4,

5, 6, 7, more."

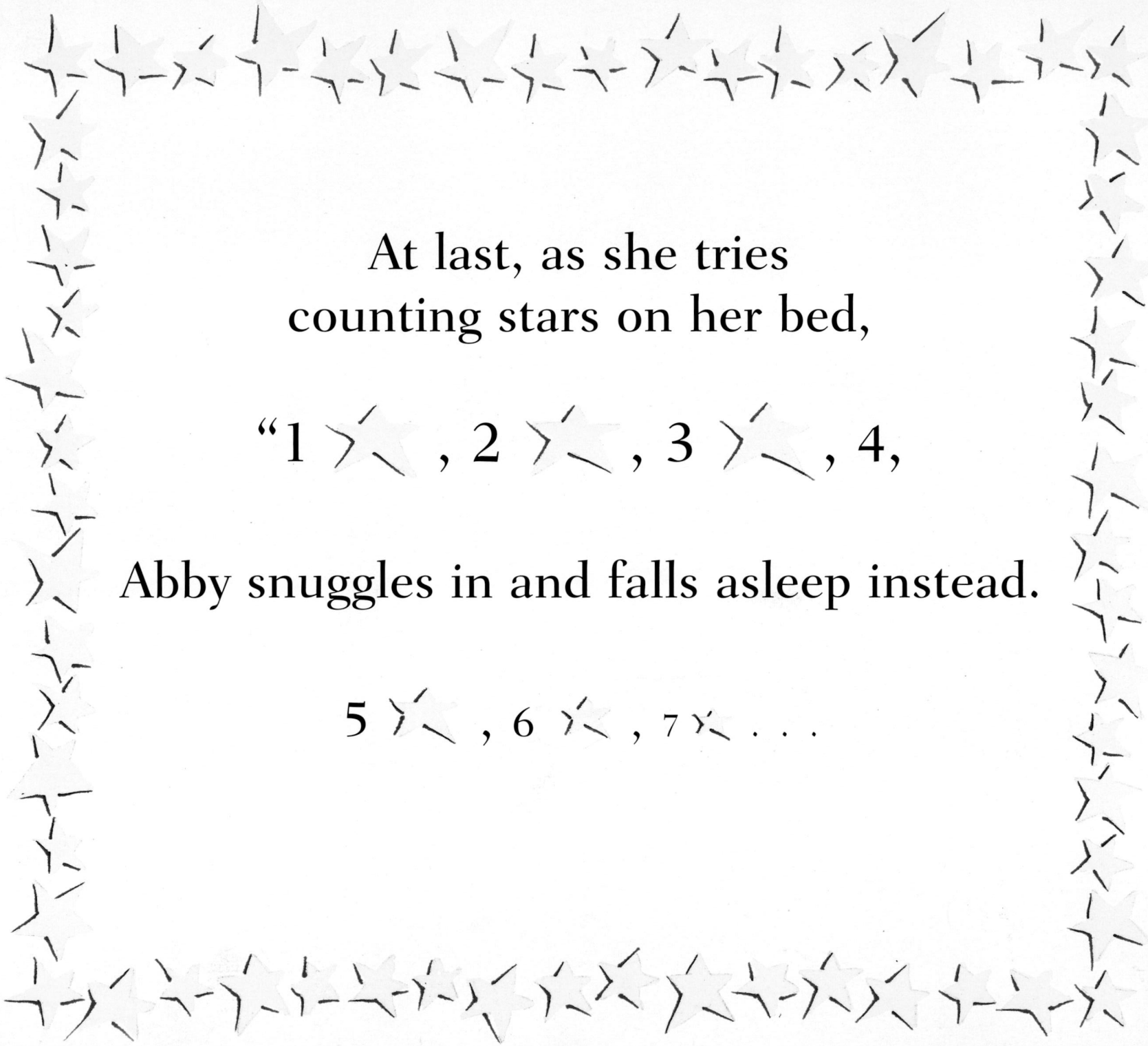

At last, as she tries
counting stars on her bed,

"1 , 2 , 3 , 4,

Abby snuggles in and falls asleep instead.

5 , 6 , 7 . . .

snore."

ORLAND PARK PUBLIC LIBRARY

For Mom

With special thanks to
Britany Sewell
and
Mariah Easton

Copyright © 1998 by Kathy Mallat
All rights reserved. No part of this book may be reproduced or transmitted in any form or by any means, electronic or mechanical, including photocopying, recording, or by any information storage and retrieval system, without permission in writing from the Publisher.
All the characters and events portrayed in this work are fictitious.
First published in the United States of America in 1998 by Walker Publishing Company, Inc.
Published simultaneously in Canada by Thomas Allen & Son Canada, Limited, Markham, Ontario

Library of Congress Cataloging-in-Publication Data
Mallat, Kathy.
Seven stars more!/Kathy Mallat
p. cm
Summary: When Abby isn't tired at bedtime, she counts sheep and almost everything else in her bedroom.
ISBN 0-8027-8675-8. —ISBN 0-8027-8676-6 (reinforced)
[1. Sleep—Fiction. 2. Bedtime—Fiction. 3. Counting]
I. Title.
PZ7.M29455Se 1998
[E]—dc21 98–6497
CIP
AC

Book design by Sophie Ye Chin

Printed in Hong Kong
2 4 6 8 10 9 7 5 3 1